OFFICIAL
KUBOTAN®
TECHNIQUES

BY

TAKAYUKI KUBOTA

and

JOHN G. PETERS, JR.

KUBOTAN® INSTITUTE

800-423-0668

Published by: **RELIAPON POLICE PRODUCTS, INC.**
3112 Seaborg Ave., Suite C
Ventura, CA 93003

ISBN 0-923401-01-6

ACKNOWLEDGEMENTS

The authors would like to thank the following people for their assistance in the preparation of this work: George W. Slade, University of Baltimore; Dr. A.J. Sullivan, Professor Emeritus, School of Public Communication, Boston University; Norman Bryden, School of Public Communication, Boston University; Robert Swan photographer, Line of Sight; Gary Egan, Executive Director, Massachusetts Criminal Justice Training Council, who pioneered the Kubotan's adoption; J.W. Simmons, Director of Extension, Sampson (NC) Technical College, who blazed a trail for the Kubotan; William E. Lavash, Director, Waltham (MA) Police Academy, who was the first to adopt the Kubotan as an integral part of recruit training; Norman Thompson, Salt Lake City (Utah) Police Department; Wilfred "Bud" Goodwin, Executive Director, Ohio Peace Officer Training Academy; Larry Plott, Director, Idaho Peace Officer Standards and Training; Michael N. Becar, Region II Training Coordinator, who graciously wrote the Preface to this book; Frank Kanekoa, Sheriff, Clark County (WA) Sheriff's Department; Michael Kestner, Training Coordinator, Clark County (WA) Sheriff's Department; Harvey Eubank, Los Angeles Police Department; M. Gary Patton, Los Angeles Police Department; John Quirke, Training Coordinator, Massachusetts Criminal Justice Training Council; J.D. Myers, (he knows where he is); Thomas J. Archambault, Michael Campbell and Frank Swartz of the Kubotan Institute; Wendy and Thea for proofreading and for making the necessary corrections; and Dianne M. Mancuso who spent countless hours typing "rough drafts". Finally, thanks to the hundreds of police, court, military and security personnel who have "street-tested" and proven the safety and the effectiveness of the techniques contained in this book.

KUBOTAN® is a registered trademark of Takayuki Kubota.

PREFACE

Officers today are constantly striving for new techniques and ideas to assist them in the controlling of situations where individuals resist arrest. Resisting may take the form of simply refusing to move, or of attempting to fight with the officer. In any arrest situation, the chances of an officer getting hurt are always high, and with today's recent trend in law enforecement to lower height and weight requirements for police applicants, as well as the number of women being hired as police officers, many officers are confronting criminals who are much larger, or who are more powerful.

Additionally, the views of society have changed toward law enforcement officers. The lack of respect toward police officers is more and more evident in the increasing number of suspects who resist arrest and who verbally chastise law enforcement officers. There does not seem to be the sense of outrage and shock voiced by society when a police officer is murdered, as shown in past decades. Those who once would have hesitated to challenge an officer's authority are no longer hesitant, and officers are finding themselves having to increasingly control suspects with physical means.

The Kubotan, developed by Master Takayuki Kubota, is a 5½ inch long cylindrical piece of plastic which, when used properly, will control a suspect, regardless of his size, by even the smallest officer. It does not appear offensive and is actually very harmless looking with one model made with a key ring. Its small size makes it ideal to be carried by uniformed officers, detectives, corrections or parole officers, or anyone else who deals in law enforcement. The Kubotan can be held in an officer's hand, under his citation book, readily available if the offense develops into an altercation. A handcuff key may be attached to the Kubotan key ring model, making the Kubotan always available when removing handcuffs from a suspect.

Another advantage of the Kubotan is that it can be carried with an officer at all times — both on and off duty — and is always readily available in a pocket, stuck in the belt, or just carried in the hand. All too often an officer is trained to use a baton or similar tool, only to find it is left in the patrol car when needed, or that the officer is not in uniform and unable to carry it.

The Kubotan shouldn't be carried unless the officer has been trained in it's use. A minimum amount of training is required to learn the six basic techniques and other applications illustrated in this manual. With proper instruction, virtually any law enforcement officer will have a tool which will enable him to do his job more effectively and safely, while minimizing injury to the suspect.

This book, with 114 photographs, contains the most complete and most comprehensive training techniques utilizing the Kubotan. It is dedicated to officer safety, to professionalism and to surviaval.

Michael N. Becar
Idaho P.O.S.T.

Michael N. Becar is a police training coordinator with the Peace Officer Standards and Training Academy (P.O.S.T.) in Boise, Idaho. He is responsible for coordinating in-service training for law enforcement officers in Southwestern Idaho.

INTRODUCTION

During the past few years, criminal justice personnel from around the globe have been using the Kubotan in their daily activities — both on and off duty. And, as you can suspect, there have been hundreds — possibly even thousands — of situations where the Kubotan has been used successfully.

We know of a few cases where, because of the Kubotan, suspect's lives were saved. In one case, a suspect had been severly beaten with a conventional baton for resisting arrest. Although badly hurt, the suspect continued to fight. An officer who had been certified in the Kubotan arrived on the scene as a responding back-up unit. Quickly, he applied the Kubotan to the suspect's wrist. Immediately, the suspect stopped struggling and "agreed" to go along with the officer. A subsequent medical examination showed that the suspect would have died, had he been hit once more with a baton.

We also know of a few cases where an officer was spared serious injury because he used the Kubotan. For example, an officer who answered a call for assistance at a hospital, was greeted upon arrival by a wild mental patient. Four other officers were chasing the patient through the hospital trying to wrestle him to the ground. The Kubotan-trained officer applied the Kubotan to the patient's wrist, subduing the mental patient. Officers have also used the Kubotan to remove people from courtrooms, jails and from similar situations.

Many officers have told us that carrying the Kubotan gives them a greater sense of security. They have commented that just carrying the Kubotan in their hand gives them an advantage over the suspect. If suddenly surprised while walking or while talking to a suspect, they are ready for action.

Another frequent comment is that unlike so many new "gimmicks" offered to them, the Kubotan is practical. Many officers carry their cruiser, handcuff, apartment or other keys on the Kubotan. It is also a handy device for "attitude adjustment", should a suspect get "frisky" during the removal of a set of handcuffs. Undercover officers cite it's harmless looking appearance and its easy concealability. And, if you are carrying the key ring model, when asked, "What is that funny looking thing?", you can honestly reply: "It's my key chain."

Key ring or plain model, the basic reason for the Kubotan's existance is *your safety.* The Kubotan can help you to better perform your duties, while increasing your safety. For example, once trained in the Kubotan you can restrain and control people without severely injuring them. Your safety is also incresased a number of ways.

First, you carry the Kubotan with you (remember your keys are on it), thus making it possible for you to immediately react to trouble. You don't need to remove it from a ring or holster to use it; it's in your hand, ready for action.

Second, should you drop it during a scuffle, no one should know how to use it. Unlike a dropped baton which can be used by most anyone to club you, to use the Kubotan a person must have been trained in it's use. The result: an important built-in safety feature.

There are numerous other ways in which the Kubotan will increase your safety; however, we'll let you discover them during your training and during your career. Remember, the single most important factor affecting your safety is *professional training*. Complete a Kubotan Institute certified training program, *before* you carry the Kubotan. The reasons: to avoid getting injured or injuring the suspect because you didn't know what you were doing, and to avoid needless litigation and law suits. The Institute's instructors are former police officers who are dedicated and trained to give you the best training available in the use of the Kubotan. All of us subscribe to the philosophy that the classroom is the best place to learn, and the only safe place to make mistakes. Once trained and certified, you too, can begin to make the Kubotan work for you.

We hope that you will never need to use the Kubotan. Should you be forced to use it, however, you will join the growing number of officers from around the world who have used it to ''adjust'' a suspect's attitude. Then you too, can tell ''war stories'' about it's effectiveness.

Takayuki Kubota
Los Angeles

John G. Peters, Jr.
Albuquerque

TAKAYUKI KUBOTA

TAKAYUKI KUBOTA, inventor of the widely-adopted Kubotan, is the Executive Director and the co-founder (with John Peters) of the internationally-recognized Kubotan Institute. He is also the Director and Vice President, repectively, of the Kubotan Institute's two sister training organizations: the Defensive Tactics Institiute, Inc. and the PR-24 International Institute, Inc.

Born in Kumamoto, Japan, in 1934, he began studying the arts of Karate and Jitsu at the age of four. His teaching career began at the age of 14 and has flourished since that time. He has been teaching police techniques for over 25 years; courses ranging from handcuffing to his world famous baton techniques. For over 22 years he has been training law enforcement personnel in the use of batons, and in his own personal techniques known as Kubo Jitsu, or the *Pen Technique.*

Holding an eighth degree black belt in Karate, a fifth degree black belt in Aikido Jitsu, a third degree black belt in Judo and a first degree black belt in Kendo, Kubota served as instructor for the Kamata-Tokyo (Japan) Police Department from 1949-1959. While there he taught Karate, baton techniques, self-defense and "tai ho jitsu". Later, with the Kamata-Tokyo Police

Department, he actively participated in the day-to-day activities of the police. It was during this period that Kubota developed, tested and refined many of his techniques.

As Kubota's reputation grew, so did his teaching. From 1958 to 1964, he instructed United States Military Police and other personnel in self-defense techniques at military bases in Japan. Kubota also served as body guard for the United States Ambassador to Japan. In 1964, he moved to the United States, and has since trained criminal justice, military and security personnel from various federal, state and local agencies.

In 1969, the Los Angeles Police Department (LAPD) placed Kubota under contract to train it's instructors at the Los Angeles Police Academy in baton, in self-defense and in apprehension techniques. In 1974, he introduced a new police baton Kendo technique to the LAPD. From October 4, through December 16, 1977, Kubota trained a special group of LAPD female police officers in his Kubotan self-defense system.

In 1974, the Federal Bureau of Investigation (FBI) sent personnel to his school to learn various self-defense and baton techniques. That same year, the FBI Academy made a 150 page manual of his techniques which is used to assist in the training of it's agents, law enforcement officers and instructors. In 1975, Kubota presented the FBI with a film on knife defensive tactics.

Kubota has also been an instructor in weaponless defense in the Police Science Program at Fullerton (CA) Junior College.

Although busy instructing, Kubota has found time to write many articles and books. His publications include: *Baton Techniques and Training* (Charles C. Thomas, publisher); *The Art of Karate* (Peebles Press, publisher); *Gosoku Ryu Karate* (Unique Publications, publisher); plus *Advanced PR-24 Baton Techniques, Handcuffing Techniques* and others too numerous to list. Kubota has a forthcoming book on Kubo Jitsu, a work showing the uses of the tonfa, the bo, the staff and other forms of stick fighting. He has also published several articles which have appeared in a variety of national and international magazines.

In addition to his writing, Kubota has also appeared in over 200 movies, commercials and television shows which include: *The Mechanic, The Killer Elite, MacArthur, Shaft in America, Operation Petticoat, Baa Baa Black Sheep, "Dinah Shore Show"* and numerous others.

A United States citizen since 1974, Kubota devotes much of his time to the teaching of Karate at his Glendale, California dojo (school). He is president and general instructor of the International Karate Association, and has affiliated schools throughout the world. In 1970, two of Kubota's students joined the U.S. Team in the entry to the World Tournament in Tokyo, Japan. In 1972, three of his students entered the World Tournament in Paris, France. Kubota has also had his students in other national and international tournaments.

In 1967, 1968 and 1969, personnel from the LAPD, all of whom were trained by Kubota, entered the following Police Olympic Tournaments and took first place: San Diego, California, Orange County, California and Phoenix, Arizona (individual champions in the National Olympics).

JOHN G. PETERS, JR.

John G. Peters, Jr. is president and founder of the Defensive Tactics Institute, Inc. He is also co-founder, with the Kubotan inventor, Takayuki Kubota, of the Kubotan Institute, a division of the Defensive Tactics Institute, Inc.

A member of the United States Secret Service Defensive Tactics Advisory Panel, John has been involved in the study of martial arts and police tactics since 1965. He holds a third degree black belt in Jiu-Jitsu and a first degree black belt in Kodokan Judo. John is also a certified international Instructor-Trainer in the Kubotan, in the side-handle baton, in the straight baton, in the Immobilizer, in the Action Control Grip, in the riot baton, in handcuffing techniques and applications, in firearm retention and disarming and in defensive tactics. He is one of the world's leading authorities on impact weapons and defensive tactics.

Educationally, Peters was awarded an Associate in Applied Science degree and a Certificate in Corrections, both *Cum Laude* from the Northern Virginia Community College; a Bachelor of Science degree, *Summa Cum Laude*, from the University of Baltimore; a Master of Science degree, from the School of Public Communication, Boston University; and a Master of Business Administration degree, *With Honors,* from Babson College. He has also done post-graduate work in governmental finance and accounting at Suffolk University.

Peters began his law enforecment career in 1969 when he was appointed to the FBI as a clerical employee. While there, he received a *Letter of Commendation* for his Judo instruction from then FBI Director, J. Edgar Hoover.

In 1972, Peters joined the Northern York County (PA) Regional Police Department as a Police Officer/Self-Defense Specialist. Later, he transferred to the York County (PA) Sheriff's Department as a Deputy Sheriff. While there, Peters spent three years on the District Attorney's Fugitive Squad.

In 1978, Peters became the Staff Executive (Civilian equivalent of Deputy Chief) of a Massachusetts police department, where he headed the Administrative Bureau (seven divisions) and the Planning and Research Unit.

Peters also served as Senior Research Associate for a Massachusetts-based criminal justice research firm. While there, he conducted extensive research into the area of management of criminal investigations, and became one of the nation's leading authorities in this field.

An avid author, he has published over fifty articles, brochures, book chapters, handbooks and text books; including: **Realistic Defensive Tactics, Defensive Tactics With Flashlight** and **Official Kubotan Techniques.** Three more books by the author are being prepared for publication during 1984.

John has also served as a management and training consultant to many criminal justice, military and security agencies including: the Los Angeles Police Department; the Seattle (WA) Police Department; the Salt Lake City (UT) Police Department; the Escambia County (FL) Sheriff's Department; the North Carolina Highway Patrol; the Massachusetts Criminal Justice Training Council; the New Mexico Law Enforcement Academy; the Smith and Wesson Academy; the United States Government; the Staff Training College; Montreal, Canada; agencies in Australia and Europe; plus many, many more.

Peters has also taught security management and other related courses in the Security Program, Northern Essex Community College. He is a member of the college's Security Advisory Board. His biographical sketch is contained in **Who's Who in the East.** He has also served over three years on the Braintree (MA) Finance Committee.

The staff of the Institute has conducted training programs for many agencies. To mention a few:

POLICE AGENCIES

- Los Angeles Police Deptartment
- California Highway Patrol
- Las Vegas Metropolitan Police Department
- Clark County (WA) Sheriff's Department
- U.S. National Park Service
- Salt Lake City Police Department
- Albuquerque Police Department
- Framingham (MA) Police Department
- North Carolina State Highway Patrol

TRAINING AGENCIES

- Massachusetts Criminal Justice Training Council
- Washington State Criminal Justice Training Commission
- Vermont Criminal Justice Training Council
- Northern Virginia Criminal Justice Academy
- Idaho P.O.S.T Academy
- New Mexico Law Enforcement Academy
- Sampson (NC) Technical College
- U.S. School of Law Enforcement

CORRECTIONAL AGENCIES

- Correctional Staff College, Quebec, Canada
- Joseph Harp (OK) Correctional Center
- Jefferson County (KY) Department of Correction
- Louisiana State Penitentiary

SECURITY AGENCIES

- Interstate Secuity (Nuclear)
- Vermont Yankee Security (Nuclear)
- Washington Public Power Supply Systems (Nuclear)
- Security Management Services
- Faulkner Hospital

TRANSPORTATION

- Massachusetts Bay Transit Authority

TABLE OF CONTENTS

DEFINITIONS

APPROPRIATE FOLLOW-UP PROCEDURES. Those procedures or techniques based upon departmental policy, rules and regulations or other legal guidelines which you select and use after effecting the arrest of an individual.

KUBOTA, TAKAYUKI. Inventor of the Kubotan. Also Executive Director of the Kubotan Institute.

KUBOTAN. A 5½ inch long cylindrical piece of plastic, approximately 5/8 inch in diameter, with the Kubotan monogram stamped on one end.

KUBOTAN BASIC CERTIFICATION. The *official* certification issued by the Kubotan Institute to those persons who successfully complete the Kubotan Institute's eight-hour basic Kubotan training course.

KUBOTAN BASIC INSTRUCTOR CERTIFICATION. The *official* certification issued by the Kubotan Institute to those persons who successfully complete the Kubotan Institute's sixteen-hour Basic Instructor training course. Once certified, the Basic Instructor may certify others in the Kubotan Institute's Basic Course.

KUBOTAN INSTITUTE. The *official* Kubotan training center, under the leadership of Kubotan inventor, Takayuki Kubota. The Kubotan Institute oversees all Kubotan training and certification.

KUBOTAN INSTRUCTOR TRAINER CERTIFICATION. The *official* certification issued by the Kubotan Institute to those persons who successfully complete the Kubotan Institute's thirty-two-hour Instructor Trainer training course. Once certified, the Instructor Trainer may certify others in the Kubotan Institute's Basic Instructor course.

OFFICIAL KUBOTAN BASIC COURSE CARD. The *official* card issued by the Kubotan Institute to those persons who successfully compete the Kubotan Basic Course. The card contains the signatures of the Executive Director and the Director of the Kubotan Institute, and the Kubotan Basic Instructor.

OFFICIAL KUBOTAN CERTIFICATION. The *official* certification issued by the Kubotan Institute to those persons who successfully complete a Kubotan Institute training course. The *official* certification **only** applies to the techniques which are taught and approved by the Kubotan Institute and used with the *official* Kubotan.

OFFICIAL KUBOTAN KEY CHAIN. A 5½ inch cylindrical piece of plastic, approximately 5/8 inch in diameter, with a key ring attached on one end, and the Kubotan monogram on the other end.

OFFICIAL KUBOTAN MANUAL. The training manual published by the Kubotan Institute. It contains **only** those techniques which are approved and taught by the instructors and the staff of the Kubotan Institute.

PETERS, JOHN. Co-founder (with Takayuki Kubota) and Director of the Kubotan Institute.

STRONG HAND. As used in this book, your gun hand. That is, if you are right handed, then your right hand is your strong hand hand; the opposite, if you are left handed.

STRONG LEG (FOOT). As used in this book, your right leg or foot, if you are right handed; the opposite, if you are left handed.

WEAK HAND. As used in this book, your non-gun hand. That is, if you draw and shoot your service weapon with your right hand, then your left hand is your weak hand.

WEAK LEG (FOOT). As used in this book, the leg or foot on the opposite side of your strong side, as previously defined.

QUESTIONS and ANSWERS

The following is a list of the most frequently asked questions about the Kubotan and the Kubotan Institute.

WHAT IS THE KUBOTAN?

Designed by **Master Takayuki Kubota,** the Kubotan is a small impact tool. The *official* Kubotan is 5½ inches long, approximately 5/8 inch in diameter, cylindrical in design with the Kubotan monogram stamped on one end. The monogram is shown below.

K

ISN'T THE KUBOTAN A SMALL YAWARA (JUDO) STICK?

NO! Shihan Kubota developed the Kubotan from his *Pen Technique.* The Kubotan **is not** taught or used as the lethal Yawara (judo) stick.

The Kubotan is easy to use, and is very effective. Through the use of various wrist locks and control holds — both causing intense pain — an attacker, regardless of size, can be restrained. The Kubotan's effectiveness is based upon the principle of pain compliance.

WHAT IS THE KUBOTAN INSTITUTE?

Internationally recognized, the Kubotan Institute is the *official* Kubotan training center.It was co-founded in 1979 by Shihan Takayuki Kubota and John G. Peters, Jr. Both are internationally recognized criminal justice, military and security trainers. The Kubotan Institiute oversees all Kubotan training and certification. It also serves as the international clearinghouse for Kubotan related information.

Under the effective and innovative leadership of Executive Director Takayuki Kubota (Kubotan inventor) the Kubotan Institute has opened offices in Albuquerque, NM and in Los Angeles, CA. These locations coupled with regional training centers and a travelling staff, have facilitated in the training of criminal justice, military and security personnel from around the world.

WHERE CAN I GET TRAINED AND CERTIFIED IN THE KUBOTAN, AND HOW MUCH DOES THE TRAINING COST?

Individual: Kubotan training courses are held on a regular basis across North America. To be notified of the next course in your area, please send your name, address and phone number to the Kubotan Institute. Finally, you may visit one of the Kubotan Institute's regional training centers. For more information write to Reliapon Police Products, Inc., 3112 Seaborg Avenue, Suite C, Ventura, California 93003.

Department: The staff of your agency may desire to have a number of personnel trained and certified in the Kubotan. If so, write to the Kubotan Institute for additional information. You'll find that unlike many training organizations and individuals, the Kubotan Institute uses a fixed fee schedule which *does not vary with class size.* This approach emphasizes *quality,* not *quantity.*

While the Kubotan Institute has salaries and overhead to pay like any organization, its staff is aware of the current budgetary constraints which have been placed upon governmental agencies. Being cost consious too, the Institute staff is aware of it's social responsibility to provide quality professional training at an affordable cost so that it is cost effective for your agency to conduct a training program.

For reduced training costs via its **SHARE-A-COURSE**® program, or for *free* training via its **HOST-A-COURSE**® program, write to the Institute on your official letterhead.

WHERE CAN I BUY A KUBOTAN?

Kubotans can be purchased from local police equipment stores, or you may purchase them directly from the Kubotan Institute.

WHO CAN TEACH THE KUBOTAN?

Only those persons who have successfully completed the Kubotan Institutes instructor certification course are authorized to teach the Kubotan. Many times, martial artists will deceptively claim their ability to teach the Kubotan. If unsure of a person's authorization and certification, ask to see his/her Kubotan Institute instructor certification. If (s)he cannot produce such certification, the person cannot *train* and *certify* you in the Kubotan.

WHY IS CERTIFICATION IMPORTANT?

Certification is a relatively simple concept, at least until you are called upon to defend it. In other words, most anyone can issue certification to you in a particular field of study or skill (this is the easy part); however, defending the criteria upon which the certification is based — especially in a court of law — may be more difficult.

Generally, certification, if it is to become accepted by most state training commissions or local police academies, must be based upon specific criteria. These criteria, many times, include the quality and intensity of the research conducted which supports the course of study. Of importance is: the specificity of findings of such research and its relationship to the course goals and objectives; the education, special training and certification, if needed by the instructor to *legitimately* teach the course; the acceptance of the material on the street and in a court of law; and in the case of training organizations, the agencies' legitimacy, credibility, professionalism and proven track record both in the field and in a court of law.

Certification is needed to *prove* that you have been deemed competent to have performed the task in question. Certification, like law making, is seldom, if ever, questioned by a court or similar body when first developed. It is usually when a problem deveops such as the striking of someone with a flashlight, that the issues of training, and more specificlly, certification will surface.

Certification implies that you were tested by a competent, legitimate and certified person who deemed you worthy of passing the course. Merely saying that you received three or four hours of baton training, or that you read the manual, *is no longer enough* when it comes to defending your actions in court. For example, cases are replete with the defense attorney questioning the officer's qualifications to use an impact tool or weapon; the instructor's qualifications; the course objectives and goals; and in the case of an outside departmental program (e.g., Kubotan program), the criteria which were used to develop the program.

Remember: An officer's certification is based upon the course content, and upon the qualifications of the instructor and the certifying body.

In essence, well documented training, testing and cetification can not only prove that an officer is competent, but also can help to insulate both you and the department from unnecessary litigation.

NOTE: The staff of the Kubotan Institute will stand behind it's training program; testifying, if necessary, in a court of law or other tribunal. The staff of the Kubotan Institute will *only* defend the *official* Kubotan training program and the *official* Kubotan.

ATTENTION
Community Relations Officers

Join the growing number of criminal justice agencies that are improving their police-community relations through the sponsoring and the teaching of civilian-oriented Kubotan self-defense classes.

The civilian program was designed and developed by the staff of the Kubotan Institute. Course material is not police related, but is designed for self-defense use by civilians.

Write, on your official letterhead, for more details:

RELIAPON POLICE PRODUCTS, INC.
3112 Seaborg Avenue, Suite C
Ventura, California 93003

TECHNIQUE ONE

SITUATION: You grasp the suspect by the wrist or the suspect grasps you by the wrist (e.g., street, barroom, domestic, correctional situations).

ACTION:

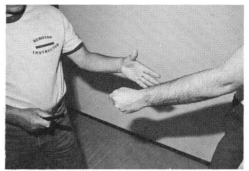

1-1

1-1. Advance toward the suspect with your weak leg (keep your firearm away from the suspect so (s)he can't grab it). Grasp the suspect's weak wrist with your weak hand, while holding the Kubotan in your strong hand.

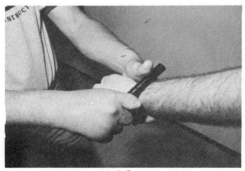

1-2

1-2. Place the Kubotan over the radial (top) wrist bone, so that it is horizontal to the ground. The left end of the Kubotan is placed under your weak thumb. The fingers on your weak hand continue to hold and to cradle the suspect's weak wrist.

1-3. Keep the Kubotan on an even plane and hook your weak thumb over the end of the Kubotan, keeping it on the inside of the suspect's forearm. Doing so will allow you to squeeze your hand more tightly. Next, squeeze your weak hand while simultaneously pushing downward with your strong hand. (Maintain even pressure on both sides of the Kubotan.) DO NOT ALLOW THE KUBOTAN TO SLIP AROUND THE WRIST, since this voids the technique.

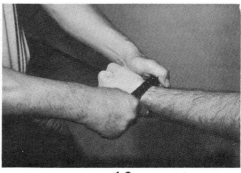

1-3

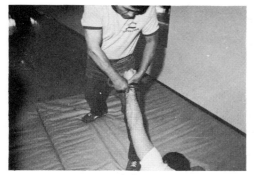

1-4. Apply pressure to the suspect's wrist, and step backward with your strong leg, pulling and driving the suspect to the ground. Maintain pressure upon the wrist for pain compliance. With the suspect lying on his/her stomach, quickly handcuff the suspects weak wrist. (NOTE: the Kubotan is still applied to the suspect's weak wrist.) Once handcuffed, use appropriate follow-up measures.

1-4

TECHNIQUE TWO

SITUATION: After advising the suspect that (s)he must go with you, (s)he refuses and begins to walk away (e.g., street, barroom, domestic or correctional situation).

ACTION:

2-1. Technique Two being applied. NOTE: the weak leg is forward which helps you to maintain a strong stance, while keeping your firearm farther away from the suspect. Finally, keep to the side of the suspect to make application easier, and to help avoid being kicked. Technique Two may be applied to either wrist of the suspect.

2-1

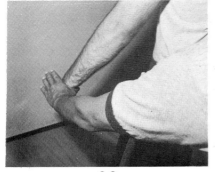

2-2. Facing the suspect's back, begin to grasp the suspect's weak wrist with your weak hand.

2-2

21

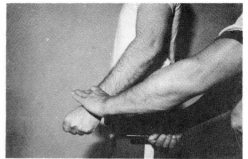

2-3. Simultaneously, push the Kubotan between the suspect's weak arm and rib area. NOTE; Holding the Kubotan by one end will make it easier to apply this technique.

2-3

2-4. After your strong hand is next to the suspect's wrist, place the Kubotan over the radial (top) wrist bone. Your thumbs are placed behind the suspect's weak wrist.

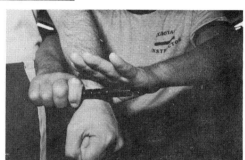

2-4

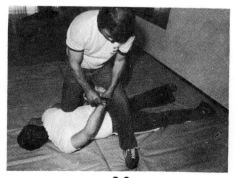

2-5. With your thumbs behind the suspect's wrist, wrap your fingers around both ends of the Kubotan. The web of your hand (the skin between your thumb and index finger) must be held tightly against each side of the suspect's weak wrist. The reason: to keep the Kubotan stable. Now, squeeze the Kubotan tightly against the suspect's radial (top) wrist bone, while slightly rotating the Kubotan toward the thumb. Maintain pressure upon the wrist for pain compliance.

2-5

2-6. While squeezing and rotating the Kubotan, simulaneously step backward with your strong foot, forcing the suspect to the ground. Once upon the ground, step over the suspect and kneel upon the suspect's right shoulder with your strong leg, thus minimizing and controlling the suspect's movement. Next, handcuff the suspect's weak wrist. NOTE: Depending upon your body type, you may wish to step over the suspect with both legs and then kneel on his/her back.

2-6·

TECHNIQUE THREE

SITUATION: You are holding or walking the suspect in a "Position of Advantage". That is, you are holding the suspect's wrist with one hand, while holding his/her bicep with the other hand. When the suspect refuses to move or makes his/her arm rgid, Technique Three may be easily applied (e.g., walking a person into the booking area, into a court room, and so forth).

ACTION:

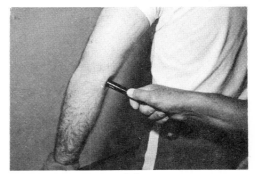

3-1

3-1. Standing slightly to the left of the suspect, grasp the suspect's weak wrist with your weak hand. Holding the Kubotan "microphone-style", push the end into the side of the suspect's elbow (ulnar nerve area). Simultaneously, bend the suspect's elbow by lifting the wrist.

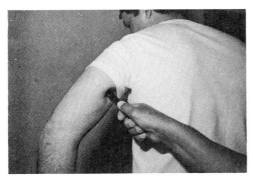

3-2

3-2. You may wish to push the Kubotan into the suspect's upper bicep area (brachial nerve area).

3-3. After the suspect's elbow is slightly bent, forcefully push the Kubotan into either elbow or the bicep area, making the suspect lean forward. Simultaneously, pull his/her weak wrist toward you.

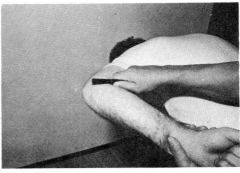

3-3

23

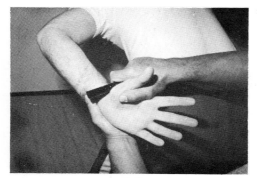

3-4.

3-4. Slide the Kubotan down the suspect's arm until it comes to rest at the base of the thumb. "Lock" your strong thumb behind the suspect's thumb. Your weak hand continues to hold the suspect's wrist.

3-5. With the Kubotan and your thumb in place, wrap your weak thumb over the end of the Kubotan. Next, squeeze the Kubotan against the suspect's thumb by drawing the Kubotan toward your strong thumb. Simultaneously, apply downward pressure with your weak thumb, by attempting to make a fist with your left hand. Remember: Keep the Kubotan across the wrist so that it doesn't move around, thus reducing the pain control hold.

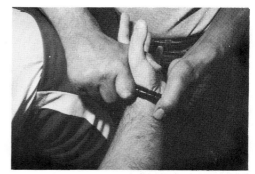

3-5

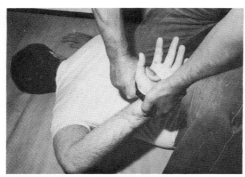

3-6

3-6. While maintaining pressure with the Kubotan upon the suspect's wrist and thumb areas, step backward with your strong foot, pulling the suspect face down onto the ground. Once down, step over the suspect and kneel upon his/her shoulder with your strong knee to minimize his/her movement, and to gain superior control.

24

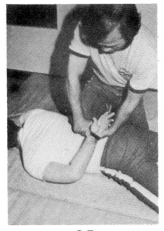

3-7. To handcuff the suspect, remove your weak hand while maintaining the Kubotan thumb lock with your strong hand. DO NOT BEND THE THUMB since it may break. Pain control is applied by squeezing it with the Kubotan. Finally, for your safety during handcuffing, do not straddle the suspect. The reasons: to maintain superior balance, and to avoid being kicked by the suspect.

3-7

TECHNIQUE FOUR *Left Hand*

SITUATION: A person tries to punch you in the face with his/her **left** hand, or attempts to grasp your shirt or badge (e.g., street, domestic, correctional, barroom settings).

ACTION:

4-1. A person attempts to strike you in the face with a **left** punch.

4-1

4-2. When you see the punching attempt, raise your left hand in preparation for blocking. Simultaneously, step to your strong side (outside the punch zone). Note the position of the Kubotan.

4-2

4-3

4-3. Side stepping the punch, apply the Kubotan to suspect's wrist area by reaching under his/her arm with your strong arm, grasping the Kubotan with your weak hand.

4-4. *Close-up of fig. 4-3 showing the Kubotan clamped over the radial (top) wrist bone.* Wrap your fingers around the ends of the Kubotan, thumbs locked under the wrist.

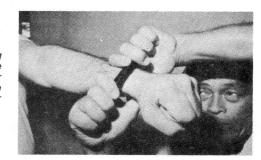

4-4

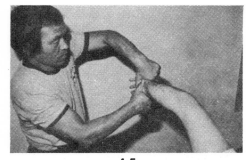

4-5

4-5. Side view showing the tight application of the Kubotan (web effect) on the suspect's wrist.

4-6. Force the suspect onto the ground, face down, by squeezing the Kubotan tightly on the wrist and by rotating it slightly forward. Simultaneously, step backward with your strong leg. Stepping backward will aid in the placement of the suspect upon the ground.

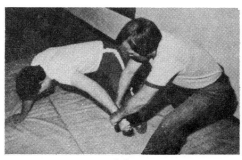

4-6

26

4-7. After the suspect is down, step over his/her waist, while maintaining pressure and pain control on the suspect's wrist.

4-7

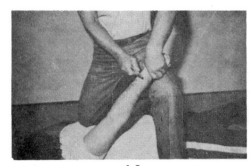

4-8

4-8. After stepping over the suspect, kneel on his/her shoulder area with your strong knee. The reason: to give you superior control, and to minimize the suspect's movement. Handcuff the suspect's weak wrist, while maintaining pressure on the wrist with the Kubotan.

TECHNIQUE FOUR *Right Hand*

SITUATION: A person tries to punch you in the face with his/her **right** hand, or attempts to grasp your shirt or badge.

ACTION:

4-9. As the person thrusts a right handed punch, snap the Kubotan in an arc across your body at head level, striking the person's wrist.

4-9

27

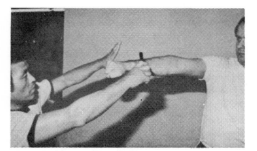

4-10

4-10. Raise both of your hands as if trying to grasp the person's wrist. Prepare to place the Kubotan over the radial wrist bone of the person's wrist, with your thumbs under his/her wrist.

4-11. Wrap your fingers around the ends of the Kubotan, clamping the person's wrist between your thumbs and the Kubotan. Squeeze tightly.

4-11

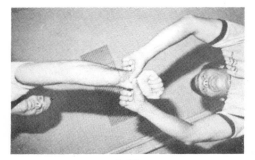

4-12. Looking upward. Note the position of the thumbs.

4-12

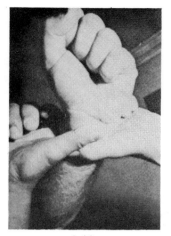

4-13. *Close-up showing the thumbs and the "gasket-like" effect made by the web of both hands.* This view also shows the tightness of the Kubotan over the person's wrist, the web of the hands creating the "gasket" against both sides of the wrist and the thumbs held firmly and pressing upward under the wrist.

4-13

4-14. Having clamped the person's wrist, pivot on your weak foot, dropping your strong foot backward completing a quarter turn. You are now to the right side of the person, which increases your safety (e.g., the person can't punch or kick at you). Force the person to the ground as shown in fig. 4-6 through 4-8.

4-14

TECHNIQUE FIVE *Strong Hand*

SITUATION: The suspect refuses to go with you after being placed under arrest. (S)He offers passive resistance and says, "If you want me, come get me."

ACTION:

5-1. Standing in an interrogation stance facing the suspect.

5-1

5-2

5-2. Only if necessary, push the Kubotan into the suspect's abdominal area to "soften" him/her. The next movement is shown in 5-3.

5-3. Generally, here is where you will begin Technique Five. Holding the Kubotan in your strong hand, begin by moving and pointing it toward the suspect's left shoulder area. Your weak hand is preparing to grasp the suspect's right arm. You remain in the interrogation stance.

5-3

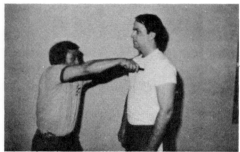

5-4

5-4. Push the Kubotan into the suspect's left shoulder area, below the clavicle bone, and to the right of the shoulder joint. Your weak hand grasps the suspect's right bicep.

5-5. Pushing into the shoulder area with the Kubotan while simultaneously pulling the suspect's right bicep toward you spin the suspect so that you will be placed behind him/her. Note the position of the Kubotan and the strong wrist.

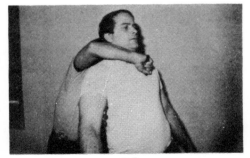

5-5

5-6

5-6. Invert the Kubotan by simply turning your strong arm so that your thumb is pointing upward. Place you strong thumb over the end of the Kubotan so that it doesn't slip through your strong hand.

5-7. Remove your weak hand from the suspect's right bicep, bringing your weak arm under the suspect's left armpit. Your strong hand is holding the Kubotan firmly against and above the suspect's pectoral area.

5-7

5-8

5-8. Grasp your strong hand with your weak hand and begin to apply pressure against the chest area with the Kubotan.

5-9. This view shows the proper position of the Kubotan. It also shows that the suspect's throat and neck areas are not being choked. **THIS IS NOT A CHOK-ING TECHNIQUE.**

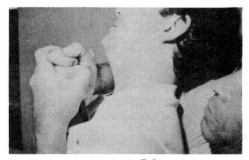

5-9

31

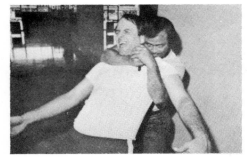

5-10. Pushing the Kubotan into the chest area while simultaneously pushing it downward will force the suspect to bend his/her knees in preparation for the takedown.

5-10

5-11. As the suspect's knees begin to bend, remove your weak hand from the Kubotan and grasp the suspect's left wrist. To insure maximum control, grasp the suspect's wrist by reaching between his/her arm and rib cage.

5-11

5-12. Force the suspect to the ground by pushing the Kubotan into the chest area, while firmly holding onto the suspect's left wrist. Do not drop onto your knees as you will lose your balance. Instead, drop your weak leg back, keeping your strong leg bent at the knee. Allow the suspect to slide down your strong leg. After (s)he is upon the ground, push your strong knee into his/her back for support.

5-12

5-13. With your strong knee pushed into the suspect's back, pull up slightly on the suspect's left wrist while pushing the Kubotan into the chest. This will force the suspect to pivot on your strong knee and roll onto his/her stomach. (The suspect will pivot toward your left.) After the suspect is prone, place your weak knee on the suspect's left shoulder. This will give you superior control and minimize the suspect's movement. Handcuff the suspect.

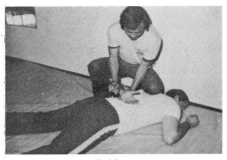

5-13

TECHNIQUE FIVE *Weak Hand*

SITUATION: Basically, the same as described in Technique Five (Strong Hand). However, appication of the previous technique may not be possible, if the subject is next to a wall or is standing beside a vehicle. Applying the technique as shown in 5-1 through 5-5 may only place the suspect's back against the wall of the vehicle. The following movements show the weak hand application.

ACTION:

5-1A. You're facing the suspect while holding the Kubotan in your weak hand.

5-1A

5-2A. Stepping to the outside of the suspect, push the Kubotan into the suspect's right shoulder blade area. Your strong hand is placed on the suspect's left shoulder.

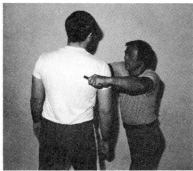

5-2A

5-3A. The side view shows the location of your strong hand. To spin the suspect, push the Kubotan into the suspect's shoulder blade area with your weak hand; simultaneously, push the suspect on his/her left shoulder using your strong hand.

5-3A

5-4A. Having turned the suspect so that you are behind him/her, bring your weak hand between his/her left arm and rib cage. Place the Kubotan on the shoulder and grasp it with either hand. You are now ready to apply those movements shown in fig. 5-6 through 5-13.

5-4A

TECHNIQUE SIX

SITUATION: *Frisking and handcuffing a suspect.* The Kubotan is very effective for pain control during a cursory "pat-down" type search. If the suspect should resist, you need only to squeeze your fingers around the suspect's fingers and the Kubotan.

ACTION:

6-1. Facing the suspect, with his/her arms raised.

6-1

6-2

6-2. Position the suspect so that (s)he cannot see you. This can generally be done by having the suspect turn away from you.

6-3. Tell the suspect to place his/her right hand on his/her neck. Then, have him/her place the left hand behind, but not tightly, against the back. Approach with your weak leg, keeping your firearm to your right rear. This will keep your firearm from becoming readily available to the suspect should (s)he suddenly turn around and try to grab it. Next, place your weak hand between the suspect's arm and back. Remember to maintain good balance, and to be watchful for sudden movements.

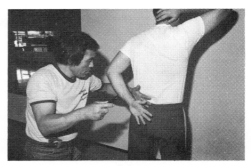

6-3

34

6-4

6-4. Insert the Kubotan between any two of the suspect's fingers. Push the Kubotan through the fingers so that it goes between your fingers too. Notice that your weak hand is palm toward you.

6-5. *Close-up of the Kubotan being placed between the suspect's fingers.* Notice that it is placed against the web of the suspect's fingers.

6-5

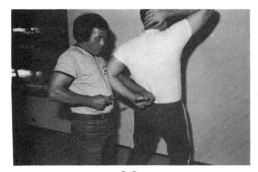

6-6

6-6. Should the suspect suddenly move, squeeze both the suspect's fingers and the Kubotan. Prepare to handcuff.

5-7. To handcuff from a standing position, hold the handcuff in your strong arm. While squeezing the suspect's left hand, reach under the suspect's right bicep with your strong hand and handcuff the wrist. Continue with appropriate follow-up measures.

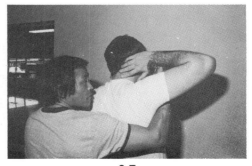

6-7

VEHICLE EXTRACTIONS

SITUATION: A motorist refuses to exit the vehicle.
ACTION:

VE1-1. Having approached the vehicle in a safely prescribed manner, open the driver's door when (s)he refuses to exit the vehicle. Next, reach toward the driver's left wrist with both of your hands. Your right hand will go under the driver's left wrist with both of your hands. Your right hand will go under the driver's left arm — between his/her bicep and rib cage. NOTE: You may hold the Kubotan in either hand; however, it is recommended that you hold it in your non-gun hand. The reason: to aid in the drawing of your firearm, if necessary.

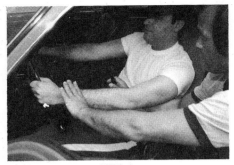

VE1-1

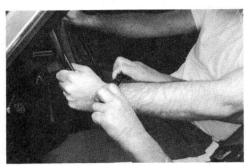

VE1-2

VE1-2. Place the Kubotan over the driver's left radial (top) wrist bone. "Lock" your thumbs under the driver's wrist eith your fingers wrapped over each end of the Kubotan. Remember to form a "gasket" with the web of each hand. This technique is similar to Technique Two.

VE1-3. With the Kubotan firmly in place, squeeze it against the driver's wrist and pull his/her hand from the steering wheel. As you pull the hand from the wheel, step back (alongside the vehicle). This will help you in removing the driver from the vehicle.

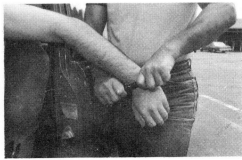

VE1-3

VE1-4

VE1-4. Step to your left and pull the driver from the vehicle. Keep pressure upon driver's wrist with the Kubotan for pain compliance.

VE1-5. Rotate the Kubotan forward toward the thumb, placing the driver upon the ground, face down. Step over the driver with your strong leg, while bending the driver's arm at the elbow.

VE1-5

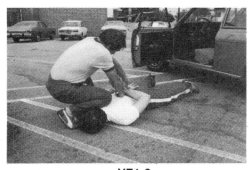

VE1-6

VE1-6. Having stepped over the driver's body with both legs, kneel, placing your knee upon the driver's right shoulder. This will provide you with a superior position, while helping to minimize his/her movement. Keeping a firm hold upon the driver's wrist with the Kubotan, pull his/her wrist toward the center of the back.

VE1-7. *View from the opposite side showing strong knee placement.* NOTE: Control the driver's right arm by placing your left ankle next to his/her bicep.

VE1-7

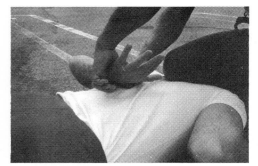

VE1-8

VE1-8. *Close-up view of holding the driver down in preparation for handcuffing.* To handcuff, remove one of your hands. Keeping pressure on the driver's wrist with the Kubotan, proceed to handcuff the driver.

VE1-9. Obviously, you cannot always place the driver alongside the vehicle: (s)he may be struck by passing traffic; you may be struck by passing traffic; or there may not be a safe opportunity to place the driver into this position (e.g., intersection, water, glass and so forth). Therefore, you must place the driver over the trunk of the vehicle after (s)he has been removed. To do so, simply pivot on your right foot and pull the driver in a semicircular motion. You may lean against the driver's side of the vehicle for support. Once the driver has been placed over the trunk, keep pressure on his/her wrist with the Kubotan

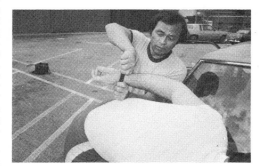

VE1-9

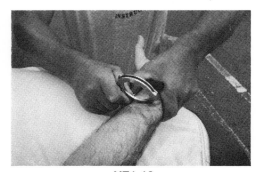

VE1-10

VE1-10. To safely handcuff the driver, step to the right side of the driver, while bending the driver's arm at the elbow. Your safety is increased as you are not in the traffic lane; your control over the suspect is greater too, due to your positioning. Next, remove one of your hands from the driver's wrist, obtain your handcuffs, and then handcuff the driver's left wrist. **Keep firm control of the driver's left wrist using the Kubotan.**

SITUATION: A motorist refuses to exit the vehicle.
ACTION:

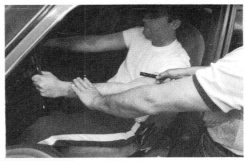

VE2-1. Having approached the vehicle in a safely prescribed manner, open the driver's door when (s)he refuses to exit the vehicle. Keeping your left leg forward and your right leg back (this keeps your firearm back too), reach toward the driver's left wrist with your left hand.

VE2-1

VE2-2

VE2-2. Grasp the driver's left wrist with your left hand. Your left hand must be palm down, with your thumb under the driver's wrist. The reasons: to increase your safety; to maintain control of the driver's arm; and to be into position for other technique applications.

VE2-3. A view from underneath shows the proper grasping of the driver's left hand. Once you have grasped the driver's wrist, forcefully push the Kubotan into the driver's left bicep or elbow area. This technique is similar to Technique Three.

VE2-3

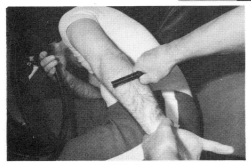

VE2-4

VE2-4. Push the Kubotan into the driver's bicep or elbow area until (s)he is forced to the right and down into the seat. Next, slide the Kubotan down the driver's forearm toward the thumb.

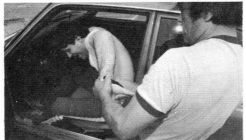

VE2-5

VE2-5. Having drawn the Kubotan into the base of the driver's left thumb, "lock" your strong thumb behind the suspect's thumb, and wrap your weak thumb over the end of the Kubotan. Your left hand continues to hold the driver's left wrist.

VE2-6. *Close-up of the Kubotan and the thumb lock.* Next, squeeze the Kubotan against the suspect's thumb by drawing it toward your right thumb. Simultaneously, apply downward pressure with your left thumb by attempting to make a fist with your left hand. Keep the Kubotan across the wrist so that it doesn't move around, thus reducing the pain control hold. After pulling the driver from the vehicle, you may use the techniques shown in fig. 3-6, 3-7 or VE1-9 and VE1-10.

VE2-6

SITUATION: A motorist refuses to exit the vehicle.
ACTION:

VE3-1. Having approached the vehicle in a safely prescribed manner, reach through the open driver's window, toward the driver's left wrist with your left hand. NOTE: To avoid being pushed into traffic should the driver suddenly thrust open the driver's door, stand to the rear of the door.

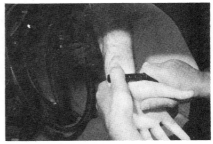

VE3-1

VE3-2

VE3-2. Grasp the driver's left wrist with your left hand. Next, reach over the driver's left arm with your right arm, placing the Kubotan upon the ulnar (bottom) wrist bone. Your right thumb should be hooked over the driver's radial (top) wrist bone.

VE3-3

VE3-3. Change the position of your left hand so that your left fingers are over the top of the driver's wrist, with your left thumb hooking the end and the underside of the Kubotan. Squeeze the Kubotan against the ulnar (bottom) wrist bone and pull the driver's left arm through the open window.

VE3-4. Staying behind the driver's door, pull the driver's arm through the open window, and advise him/her to open the driver's door from the outside with his/her right hand. (S)He will also use the right hand to unbuckle the seat belt or the shoulder harness. As the driver pushes open the door, move to your left while keeping constant pressure on the wrist with the Kubotan.

CAUTION: Watch the driver's right hand. There have been situations where drivers have had firearms mounted on the inside of the door, beneath the window.

VE3-4

VE3-5

VE3-5. After the driver has exited the vehicle, have him/her bend at the knees and put the right arm behind the back. Remove the Kubotan from the driver's left wrist, applying it to the driver's right wrist. The Kubotan is placed against the driver's ulnar (bottom) wrist bone with your thumb hooked over the Radial (top) wrist bone. Squeeze the Kubotan against the driver's right wrist causing compliance.

VE3-6. Remove your left hand from the driver's left wrist. Grasp the end of the Kubotan with your left finger, thumb on top of the driver's wrist. Squeeze, causing pain compliance, and then walk the driver to the trunk. After the driver has leaned over the trunk, release one of your hands, obtain your handcuffs, and handcuff the driver. Use appropriate follow-up procedures.

VE3-6

PASSIVE RESISTANCE - Sitting in a Chair

SITUATION: A person refuses to stand. (S)he might be sitting in a chair or similar piece of furniture (e.g., domestic, barroom, correctional settings).

ACTION:

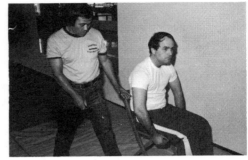

SI-1

SI-1. Approach the person who is sitting in a chair from either the right or the left rear corner. Notice that the suspect has grasped the sides of the chair seat with both his hands.

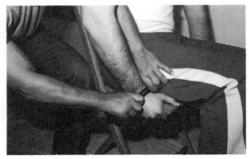

SI-2

SI-2. To remove the person, apply Technique Two. Reach between the person's right arm and rib cage with your left arm, while the right hand places the Kubotan across the suspect's right wrist. Your fingers wrap around the ends of the Kubotan, with your thumbs "locked" behind the wrist.

SI-3. Technique Two as applied on the person's left side.

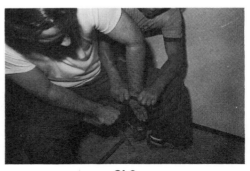

SI-3

SI-4. The Kubotan applied, squeeze tightly causing pain compliance. Pull the person's hand from the chair seat and step back. Use appropriate follow-up measures.

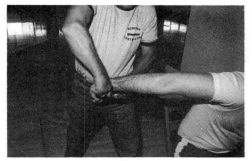

SI-4

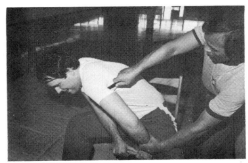

SI-5

SI-5. Technique Three may also be used to remove the person from the chair. Grasp the person's left wrist with your weak hand. Forcefully, push the Kubotan into the person's bicep or elbow. As the suspect leans forward, pull the left wrist from the chair seat. Next, slide the Kubotan down the suspect's forearm untill it reaches the base of the thumb. Obtain a thumb lock as shown and described in 3-4. Use appropriate follow-up measures.

PASSIVE RESISTANCE - Grasping a Chair

SITUATION: A person grabs a chair back or similar item and refuses to submit to an arrest (e.g., domestic, barroom, correctional settings).

ACTION:

ST-1. Approach the person from either the right or the left rear corner. From the person's right, reach between his/her forearm and rib cage with your weak hand. Keep your left foot forward, right leg back. The reasons: to keep good balance and to keep your firearm away from the person.

ST-1

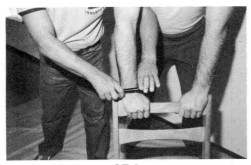

ST-2

ST-2. Apply Technique Two to the person's wrist. Place the Kubotan over the person's right radial (top) wrist bone. Wrap your fingers around the ends of the Kubotan, keeping your thumbs behind the person's wrist.

ST-3. *Side view of the Kubotan placed over the person's wrist.* Notice the "gasket-type" effect which is produced by the web of the hands. Next, squeeze the Kubotan tightly, and pull the person's hand from the chair back. After the suspect's hand is removed, rotate the Kubotan toward his/her thumb and handcuff as shown and described in fig. 2-6.

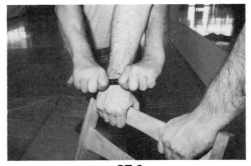

ST-3

PASSIVE RESISTANCE - Grasping a Pole

SITUATION: A suspect, inmate or other person grasps a cylindrical object, such as a jail bar, and refuses to let go.

ACTION:

JB-1. Approach the person from a position of advantage. Keep your firearm away and keep good balance.

JB-1

JB-2

JB-2. Place the Kubotan over the person's right wrist with your strong hand, while reaching under the person's forearm with your weak hand.

JB-3. Apply the Kubotan across the person's radial (top) wrist bone: Technique Two. Your thumbs are placed under the person's ulnar (bottom) wrist bone, and your fingers wrap around both ends of the Kubotan. Remember to produce the "gasket" which will keep the Kubotan stable.

JB-3

JB-4

JB-4. Squeeze the Kubotan tightly, and rotate it toward the person's thumb. Next, pull the person's wrist down and toward your waist, while taking a step backward.

JB-5

JB-5. Pull the person's arm toward the ground while squeezing and rotating the Kubotan (rotate it toward the themb). This will cause the person's knees to bend.

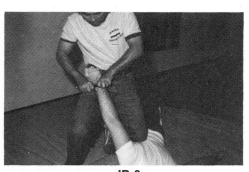

JB-6

JB-6. Continue pressure with the Kubotan while placing the person upon the ground face down. Once upon the ground, place your weak knee upon the person's right shoulder blade to control his/her movement. Keep pressure on the person's wrist with the Kubotan. Straighten the person's arm (no bend at the elbow) so that you can keep better control of the person.

JB-7. To handcuff, release the person's wrist with one of your hands, obtain your handcuffs, and then handcuff the restrained wrist. For additional support, you may place the person's forearm upon your strong leg. Keep your strong leg bent at the knee for good balance and to ease in the placing of your weak knee upon the person's right shoulder blade.

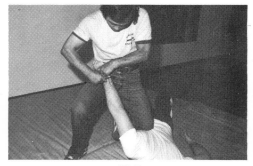

JB-7

46

PASSIVE RESISTANCE - Sitting on the Ground

SITUATION: A person is sitting on the ground, arms folded, and refuses to either stand and/or leave when you ask him/her to do so (e.g., demonstrators, strikers, passive resisters, intoxicated persons, and so forth).

ACTION:

DE-1

DE-1. Approach the person from behind, holding the Kubotan in your strong hand.

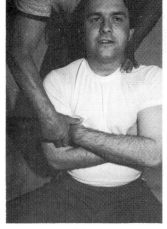

DE-2

DE-2. Place the Kubotan under the person's ulnar (bottom) wrist bone, with your strong thumb placed over his/her Radial (top) wrist bone.

DE-3. In a few cases, you may find the person's hands and wrists are so tightly lodged under the arm pits, that it's impossible to place the Kubotan under the wrist. The remedy: push the edge of the Kubotan into the top of the person's hand or wrist. When the person's hand moves away from the arm pit, insert the Kubotan under the wrist.

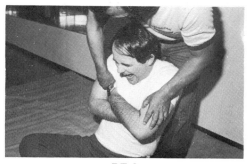

DE-3

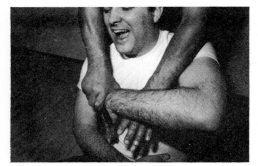

DE-4

DE-4. The Kubotan in place, pull the person's arm slightly away from the chest so that your weak arm can be placed between the person's chest and forearm.

DE-5. Grasp the Kubotan with your weak hand, wrapping your fingers around its end with your thumb "locked" behind the person's wrist.

The Kubotan, most likely, will now be positioned across the top of the hand. Squeeze tightly, and pull the person's arm away and to the left.

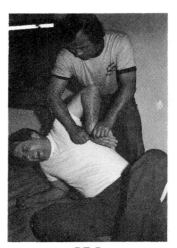

DE-5

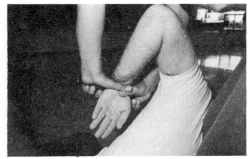

DE-6

DE-6. *Rear view showing proper thumb placement.* Once applied, you may have the person stand, or you may place him/her upon the ground, face down, for hand-cuffing.

DE-7. Another remedy is to grasp the person's left wrist with your weak hand. Then, push the end of the Kubotan into the elbow or bicep. After the arm is free, you may apply Techniques Two or Three.

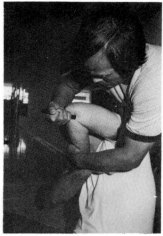

DE-7

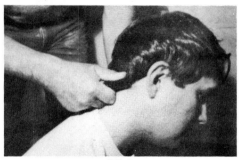

DE-8

DE-8. You may also push the Kubotan into the person's back, just below the shoulder blade. Cupping the person's chin in your weak hand, push the Kubotan into the back and with an upward "scooping" motion, lift the person to his/her feet.

DE-9. You may also "pinch" the hair between your thumb and the Kubotan. Simply place the short hairs of the neck between the Kubotan and your thumb and then lift.

DE-9

DE-10. A very effective technique is to "clothes pin" the person's ear. Simply "pinch" the ear between the thumb and the Kubotan. Your weak hand should "cup" the person's chin and assist him/her from the sitting position.

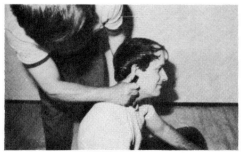

DE-10

PASSIVE RESISTANCE - Lying on the Ground

SITUATION: A person lying on his/her back refuses to either stand and/or leave when you ask them to do so (e.g., demonstrators, passive resisters, strikers, intoxicated persons, and so forth).

ACTION:

LY-1. Approach the person on an angle to minimize the risk of being kicked. Generally, your approach will be made by walking toward the shoulder. As shown, the Kubotan is in your strong hand.

LY-1

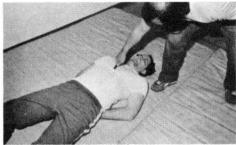

LY-2

LY-2. Bend over the person's upper body and push the edge of the Kubotan into the chest. Keep pressure on it until the person's arms reach toward the Kubotan.

LY-3. As the person reaches for your hand or for the Kubotan, grasp his/her left arm with your weak hand.

LY-3

LY-4

LY-4. Apply Techniques Two, Three or Four to the person's wrist. You may then lift the person from the ground, or roll him/her over — face down — for hand cuffing. To roll the person, quickly walk around his/her head untill the person is face down.

BEARHUG DEFENSE

SITUATION: A person refuses to stand (S)he might be sitting in a chair or similar piece of furniture (e.g., domestic, barroom, correctional settings).

ACTION:

BH-1. Arms pinned by your side, raise your hands by bending your arms at the elbow. Press the end of the Kubotan into the top of the attacker's hand.

BH-1

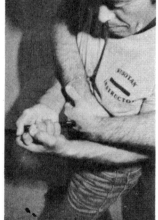

BH-2

BH-2. Close-up showing the proper method of pushing the Kubotan into the attacker's hand.

BH-3. If your arms are pinned so tightly that you can't raise your hands, step to your left (Kubotan is in your right hand). Then, thrust the Kubotan into the attacker's lower abdominal area. NOTE: This technique will have little impact, if the attacker is wearing a long, heavy coat.

BH-3

FULL NELSON DEFENSE

SITUATION: A person manages to place you into a Full Nelson (e.g., street, domestic, barroom, correctional settings).

ACTION:

FN-1. When the Full Nelson hold is applied, lift your arms upward.

FN-1

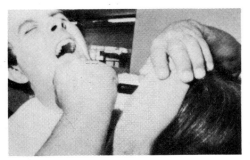

FN-2

FN-2. Grasp one of the attacker's hands with your weak hand, while pressing an end of the Kubotan into the attacker's hand.

FN-3. As the attacker loosens his/her grip, step forward holding onto the attacker's hand. Simultaneously, lower your weak arm, and push the Kubotan into the attacker's stomach or lower abdominal area.

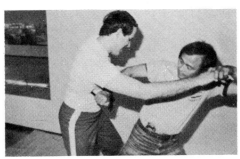

FN-3

REAR CHOKE DEFENSE

SITUATION: An attacker chokes you from behind (e.g., street, barroom, domestic, correctional settings).

ACTION:

CH-1. As soon as you're choked, turn your chin into the "V" of the attacker's elbow. The reason: so you can breathe. Then, forcefully press one end of the Kubotan into the attacker's forearm muscles and tendons. Keep firm pressure on this area until the attacker releases his/her grip.

CH-1

KICKING DEFENSE

SITUATION: A person attempts to kick you using a front snap kick (e.g., street, barroom, domestic, correctional settings).

ACTION:

KI-1. When the person begins to kick with his/her right foot, quickly step to your left. This is easily done by stepping back with your right foot while pivoting on the ball of your left foot. Simultaneously, snap the Kubotan into the kicker's shin area.

KI-1

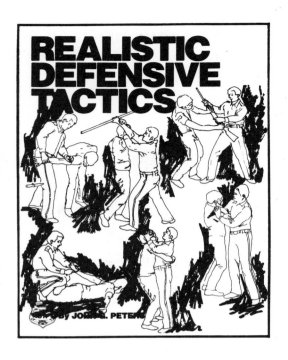

REALISTIC DEFENSIVE TACTICS has been called the **Bible** of modern, practical, effective and street-proven self-defense techniques by many working police officers. Written by internationally-recognized defensive tactics instructor, John G. Peters, Jr., this manual is a **reading must** before you confront your next suspect.

The author has given you the best of his many years of training in the martial arts and police techniques in a well-thought-out and highly-graphic training manual. This state-of-the-art training manual contains **over 500** clear line drawings which take you step-by-step through a variety of effective and street-proven techniques. The author covers such timely topics as handcuffing, searching, vehicle extractions, weapon disarming, club disarming, removal of passive resisters, control and restraint techniques, plus much more. The techniques are easy to learn, easy to execute and hard to defeat.

REALISTIC DEFENSIVE TACTICS is totally practical for today's street officer. Foreward by Massad Ayoob of the Lethal Force Institute. 8¼'' x 10¾'', softcover, 114 pages.

DEFENSIVE TACTICS WITH FLASHLIGHTS is the most complete text ever to be written on the **defensive** uses of the flashlight. The author, John G. Peters, Jr., is an internationally-recognized defensive tactics instructor, and is president of the Defensive Tactics Institute, Inc.

This state-of-the-art training manual with it's 20 chapters and over 250 clear line drawings, takes you step-by-step through flashlight retention techniques, flashlight tactics for survival, defensive blocking techniques, vehicle extractions, weapon retention techniques, plus much more.

Chapter II, **FLASHLIGHTS: SELECTING THE ONE THAT BEST FITS YOUR NEEDS,** is a reading must **before** you select a flashlight.

In Chapter XIX, **FLASHLIGHTS AND THE LAW,** the author discusses the law surrounding the use of force, the impact of flashlight policy, rules and regulations on officers who carry or are issued the flashlight, plus much more. You won't want to miss the flashlight cases where police officers were sued for having allegedly misused the flashlight; many were acquitted, but some went to jail.

Also presented are the latest in shooting techniques with the aid of a flashlight. Truly long overdue, it's a one-of-a-kind text. Foreword by Joe C. Mollo of the San Francisco Police Department. 6'' x 9'', softcover, 180 pages.

KUBOTAN®
TRAINING

If you or your agency would like to receive training in the defensive uses of the Kubotan, please write to:

RELIAPON POLICE PRODUCTS, INC.
3112 Seaborg Ave., Suite C
Ventura, CA 93003
USA

800-423-0668